AXEL M. MOSLER

TOSCANA PANORAMA

Text by Volker Skierka

EDITION**PANORAMA**

TOSCANA

Der Himmel auf Erden

Zum Glück gibt es die Toskana schon. Sonst müsste jemand den Allmächtigen überreden, die Schöpfungsgeschichte um ein paar Überstunden zu verlängern, damit, bitteschön, der Welt in der Gegend um die Städte Florenz und Siena noch jene Landschaft hinzugefügt werde. Und die einzigartig passenden kulturhistorischen Beigaben, welche insbesondere die Frührenaissance beizeiten geschaffen hat, sollten dabei nicht vergessen werden. Ohne dieses Hügelland, das mal als breiter Sandstrand und mal als steile Felsküste zum Tyrrhenischen Meer abfällt, diese sanft gewellte, von Zypressen, Pinien und edlen Weinstöcken bestandene Gegend, den Chianti-Classico, auf dessen Kuppen hier und dort, wie hingetupft, malerische Höfe, Kastelle oder Dörfer sitzen, ohne die Maremma und die Crete würde unserer Erde wahrhaftig etwas Wichtiges fehlen. Die Harmonie und der Einklang der Landschaft und der Orte mit sich und dem Himmel, den Menschen und den Stimmungen der Tages- und der Jahreszeiten ziehen den Betrachter selten irgendwo so sehr in Bann wie in der Toskana. Hier möchte man sein.

Der kulturelle und ästhetische Reichtum der Toskana, von Menschen und der Natur geschaffen, geformt und bewahrt, ist so reichhaltig und vielfältig wie kaum irgendwo sonst. Er verleitet – zugegeben – leicht zu Schwärmerei und Übertreibung. Quell des Weltwunders Toskana war und ist Florenz. Allein, die gesellschaftlichen und kulturellen

TUSCANY

Heaven on Earth

Tuscany, thankfully, already exists. Otherwise someone would have to convince the almighty to lengthen the story of creation with a few hours of overtime, so that, if you please, in the region around the cities of Florence and Siena just that very landscape would be added to the world, and the uniquely compatible historico-cultural adjuncts which the Early Renaissance in particular had created in its time, should thereby not be forgotten. Without this hill country, sloping off in some places into the Tyrrhenian Sea as a broad, sandy beach or as steep rocky coastline, without this gently rolling country with stands of cypresses, pines and noble vines, Chianti-Classico, upon whose peaks here and there, as if dabbed with brushstrokes, picturesque farmsteads, castles or villages are perched, without Maremma and La Crete, our Earth would be seriously lacking something. The harmony and unison of the landscape and localities with each other and with the sky, the people and the mood of the time of day and of the seasons, seldom put the observer anywhere so much under their spell as in Tuscany. It is here where one wants to be.

The cultural and aesthetic wealth of Tuscany, created, formed and maintained by the people and by nature itself, is so rich and varied like almost nowhere else. It deceives – admittedly slightly – to create over-enthusiasm and exaggeration. The source of this wonder-of-the-world Tuscany was, and is, Florence. The societal and cultural

LA TOSCANE

Le paradis sur terre

Heureusement que la Toscane existe, sinon il faudrait convaincre le Tout-Puissant de faire des heures supplémentaires et de revoir la Genèse pour ajouter au monde ses paysages autour de Florence et de Sienne. Sans oublier les compléments historico-culturels créés en temps voulu, en particulier au début de la Renaissance, qui s'adaptent au cadre de manière unique. Sans ce pays de collines qui descend vers la mer Tyrrhénienne, ici sous forme de large plage de sable, là sous forme de falaise abrupte, cette région doucement ondulée plantée de cyprès, de pins et de vignes nobles – le Chianti Classico –, sur les crêtes de laquelle apparaissent ici et là des fermes pittoresques, des forts romains ou des villages, sans la Maremme et le Crete, il manquerait à notre terre quelque chose d'essentiel. Il est rare que l'harmonie régnant entre le paysage et les lieux, l'accord parfait de ceux-ci avec le ciel, avec les gens et les humeurs au fil des heures et des saisons fascinent autant le spectateur. C'est ici, en Toscane, que l'on aspire à être.

Créée par la nature et la main de l'homme, formée et préservée, la richesse culturelle et esthétique de la Toscane est si opulente et variée qu'il est rare de trouver sa pareille. Elle incite, c'est vrai, à l'enthousiasme sentimental et à l'exagération. L'origine de cette merveille du monde qu'est la Toscane est et reste Florence. Les seules impulsions socioculturelles émanant de cette ville il y a cinq, six, sept siècles ont aussi préparé les Lumières. A l'époque, au 14e siècle,

TOSCANA

El cielo en la Tierra

Afortunadamente la Toscana ya existe. De no ser así, alguien tendría que convencer al Todopoderoso de que prolongara unas horas más la historia de la creación para que –por favor– enriqueciera al mundo con este paisaje en la región que se extiende en los alrededores de las ciudades de Florencia y Siena. Y sin olvidar las añadiduras histórico-culturales, que tan extraordinariamente se adecuan a este entorno, creadas sobre todo por el renacimiento temprano. Sin esta región montañosa, que desciende hasta el mar Tirreno a veces como playa de arena ancha y a veces como costa rocosa acantilada, sin esta región suavemente ondulada cubierta de cipreses, pinos piñoneros y nobles cepas –por ejemplo, el chianti clásico– sobre cuyas cimas descansan, aquí y allá, como motas en el paisaje, fincas pintorescas, castillos o pueblos, sin Maremma y sin Crete, sin todo ello, a nuestra Tierra verdaderamente le faltaría algo importante. Difícilmente encontraremos otro paraje en el que la armonía y la consonancia del paisaje y de pueblos entre sí y con el cielo, con las personas y con los distintos estados de ánimo de las horas del día y las estaciones del año sean capaces de embelezar tanto al observador como en la Toscana. Uno quiere estar aquí.

Las riquezas cultural y estética de la Toscana creadas, formadas y conservadas por el hombre y la naturaleza son tan copiosas y variadas como no existe casi en ningún otro lugar. Debemos admitir que esta abundancia induce

LA TOSCANA

Il paradiso in terra

Per fortuna la Toscana già esiste. Altrimenti bisognerebbe convincere il Padreterno a fare gli straordinari della Creazione per arricchire il mondo, dalle parti di Firenze e Siena, con i suoi celebri paesaggi. E non vanno dimenticati poi i tanti doni che straordinariamente vi si armonizzano e che la storia dell'arte, in particolare il primo Rinascimento, ha saputo apportare. Senza questo territorio collinare che digrada sul Tirreno a volte sottoforma di spiaggia sabbiosa, a volte in forma di ripida scogliera, senza questo territorio dolcemente ondulato e ricco di cipressi, pini, vigneti, la zona del Chianti Classico sui cui dossi sorgono corti, castelli e villaggi pittoreschi e anzi quasi pittorici, senza la Maremma e la Crete Senesi, al nostro pianeta mancherebbe di certo qualcosa di importante. Sono poche le regioni al mondo in cui, come in Toscana, l'osservatore è affascinato da una simile armonia di campagna e città, cielo, persone, atmosfere che si alternano nel corso delle giornate e delle stagioni. Qui vale la pena di stare.

La ricchezza culturale ed estetica della Toscana, creata, formata e preservata dall'uomo e dalla natura, è abbondante e variegata come in nessun'altra regione del mondo. Bisogna ammettere che è facile lasciarsi trascinare dall'entusiasmo fino all'esagerazione. La fonte di questa meraviglia del mondo è Firenze. Gli stimoli sociali e culturali che di qui partirono cinquecento, seicento e anche settecento anni

Impulse, welche vor fünf-, sechs-, siebenhundert Jahren von hier ausgingen, waren auch Wegbereiter der Aufklärung. Damals, im 14. Jahrhundert, galt Florenz, die „Schöne am Arno", mit ihren 100 000 Einwohnern als reichste Stadt des Abendlandes. Jene Geschlechter, die von hier aus herrschten, Kriege führten, Handel trieben, in die Welt aufbrachen, ihre Gedanken aufschrieben, malten, formten, bauten und Florenz bedeutend machten, waren keine Pharaonen, keine Kaiser oder legendäre Eroberer und Heerführer. Es waren Intellektuelle, humanistisch gebildete, zugleich aber äußerst machtbewusste Geschäftsleute. Sie standen in ihren ökonomischen, staatsbürgerlichen und – vagen – demokratischen Ambitionen in der guten Tradition der altertümlichen Hochkulturen wie jenen der griechischen und römischen Antike.

Florenz, vor knapp 2000 Jahren zu Füßen der einst wichtigen Etruskersiedlung Fiesole gegründet, aufgestiegen im 9. Jahrhundert als Markgrafschaft unter Karl dem Großen, Anfang des 13. Jahrhunderts Zentrum des mörderischen Kampfes zwischen den papsttreuen Welfen (Guelfen) und den kaisertreuen Hohenstaufen (Ghibellinen), wurde früh eine bürgerliche Republik. Sie sollte über eine Zeitspanne von rund 400 guten wie schlechten Jahren von einer Großfamilie beherrscht werden: den Medici. Die waren nicht zimperlich, wenn es um die Durchsetzung ihrer Interessen ging und schreckten auch vor Manipulationen und Schlimmerem nicht zurück, wenn es ihnen nutzte oder sie ihre Macht bedroht sahen. Der erste Medici war Cosimo der Ältere (1389–1464), ein begnadeter

impulses alone, which emanated from here five, six, seven hundred years ago, were forerunners of the enlightenment. At that time, in the 14th century, Florence, 'the beauty on the Arno', with its 100,000 inhabitants, was considered to be the richest city in all the occident. Those noble families which ruled from the city, made war, traded, set forth into the wide world, wrote down their thoughts, painted, formed, erected buildings and made Florence important, were not pharaohs, nor emperors nor legendary discoverers or field marshals. They were intellectuals who were taught in humanism, but at the same time however, extremely power-conscious merchants. They lived out their economic, civic-political and (vaguely) democratic ambitions in the fine tradition of the ancient advanced civilisations like those in Greek and Roman antiquity.

Florence, founded almost 2000 years ago further down in the valley below the once important Etruscan settlement of Fiesole, developed in the 9th century into a margravate under Charlemagne. At the beginning of the 13th century it was the centre of the bloody fighting between the papally-loyal Welfs (Guelphs) and supporters loyal to the imperial House of Hohenstaufen (Ghibellines), and it soon became a civic republic. It was to be ruled, over a period of about 400, good as well as bad, years by a princely family: the Medicis. They were not squeamish when asserting their interests and did not flinch from utilising manipulations and worse, when it was to their advantage or when they saw their power threatened. The first Medici was Cosimo the Elder (1389–1464), an exceptionally gifted

Florence « la Belle » avec ses cent-mille habitants était considérée comme la ville la plus riche de l'Occident. Ceux qui ont régné ici, guerroyé, fait du commerce, qui sont partis explorer le monde, qui ont écrit leurs pensées, qui ont peint, créé, construit et contribué à la grandeur de Florence, n'étaient ni des pharaons ni des empereurs ou des conquérants et généraux mythiques. Ils étaient des intellectuels, des hommes d'affaires ayant reçu une éducation humaniste, tout en étant extrêmement autoritaires. Leurs ambitions économiques, civiques et – vaguement – démocratiques, les plaçaient dans la lignée de la bonne tradition des grandes civilisations antiques telles que la grecque et la romaine.

Fondée il y a près de deux mille ans au pied de Fiesole, une cité étrusque autrefois importante, devenue au 9e siècle un margraviat sous Charlemagne, au cœur du conflit mortel entre les Guelfes soutenant le pape et les Gibelins fidèles à l'empereur Hohenstaufen au début du 13e siècle, Florence devient rapidement une république civile. Quatre siècles durant, elle sera, bon an mal an, gouvernée par la grande famille des Médicis. Ceux-ci n'étaient pas très tendres quand il s'agissait d'imposer leurs intérêts, n'hésitant pas à recourir à la manipulation ou pire encore lorsqu'ils le jugeaient utile ou voyaient leur pouvoir menacé. Le premier fut Cosme l'Ancien (1389 – 1464), un commerçant génial et un ami des beaux-arts. Aimé du peuple comme chef de l'opposition contre l'oligarchie, il a posé les bases de la puissance et de la richesse de ses descendants. « Nous ne sommes ni des rois ni des princes à Florence. Aucun

fácilmente al apasionamiento y a la exageración. La fuente de la maravilla del mundo llamada Toscana fue y es Florencia. Los impulsos sociales y culturales que salieron de allí hace quinientos, seiscientos, setecientos años también fueron precursores de la Ilustración. En aquella época, en el siglo XIV, Florencia, la "bella del Arno", con sus 100.000 habitantes, era considerada la ciudad más rica de occidente. Aquellas familias que desde ese lugar gobernaron, hicieron guerras, comerciaron, marcharon a recorrer el mundo, plasmaron sus ideas y pensamientos por escrito, pintaron, formaron, construyeron e hicieron de Florencia una ciudad prestigiosa no fueron ni faraones, ni emperadores, ni conquistadores legendarios o jefes de ejércitos. Fueron intelectuales, hombres de negocios con formación humanista y, al mismo tiempo, con una extraordinaria conciencia de su poder. En lo que se refiere a sus ambiciones económicas, cívicas y vagamente democráticas, se encontraban dentro de la buena tradición de las grandes civilizaciones del pasado como, por ejemplo, la antigua Grecia y la antigua Roma.

Florencia fue fundada hace unos 2000 años a los pies de la otrora importante población etrusca de Fiesole. En el siglo IX, durante el reinado de Carlomagno, fue elevada a la categoría de margraviato. Más tarde, a principios del siglo XIII, fue el centro de las luchas mortales entre la facción de los güelfos, fieles al Papa, y la de los gibelinos, fieles al emperador de la casa de Hohenstaufen. Sin embargo, muy pronto se convirtió en una república civil. Durante un periodo de aproximadamente 400 años, en las

fa, prepararono il terreno all'Illuminismo. All'epoca, nel XIV secolo, la "Bella dell'Arno", con i suoi 100.000 abitanti, era considerata la più ricca città dell'Occidente. Le dinastie che da qui signoreggiavano, guerreggiavano, commerciavano, partivano per terre lontane, scrivevano le proprie idee, dipingevano, plasmavano, erigevano edifici rendendo grande Firenze, non erano dinastie di faraoni, imperatori, conquistatori leggendari o comandanti militari. Si trattò piuttosto di intellettuali, mercanti di formazione umanistica ma al tempo stesso consapevoli del proprio potere. Con le loro ambizioni economiche, borghesi e vagamente democratiche si collocarono nella buona tradizione delle antiche culture alte, come quella greca e quella latina.

Firenze, fondata quasi 2000 anni fa ai piedi dell' insediamento etrusco di Fiesole, un tempo significativo, assurta nel IX secolo alla dignità di marca sotto Carlo Magno, teatro nel XIII secolo della cruenta lotta tra Welfen (Guelfi), fedeli al Papa, e Hohenstaufen (Ghibellini), fedeli all'Imperatore, fu una delle prime repubbliche borghesi. Per un arco di 400 anni e in una grande alternanza di sorti fu dominata da una grande famiglia: i Medici. Questi non andavano per il sottile quando si trattava di affermare i propri interessi e non avevano remore a dar vita a manipolazioni o pratiche ancor peggiori quando vi vedevano un vantaggio o il loro potere era messo in pericolo. Il primo dei Medici fu Cosimo il Vecchio (1389 – 1464), un mercante assai dotato amante delle belle arti. Amato dal popolo in quanto capofila dell'opposizione all'oligarchia, fu lui a gettare le basi del potere e della

Geschäftsmann und Freund der schönen Künste. Beim Volk beliebt als Anführer der Opposition gegen die Oligarchie, legte er den Grundstock für die Macht und das Vermögen seiner Nachfahren. „Wir sind nicht Könige, nicht Fürsten in Florenz. Kein Pergament verbrieft uns unsere Größe. Wir herrschen ohne Krone, von Natur, aus uns", lässt Thomas Mann in seinem einzigen Schauspiel „Fiorenza" Cosimos Enkel, den großen Lorenzo de Medici (1449–1492), „Il Magnifico" (Der Prächtige) genannt, auf dem Sterbebett zu seinem Sohn Piero sagen. Und ihn dann ermahnen: „Wir wurden groß in uns, durch Fleiß, durch Kampf, durch Zucht: da staunte die träge Menge und fiel uns zu. Doch solche Herrschaft, mein Sohn will täglich neu errungen sein. … Denkst Du zu ruhen, und tatenlos zu glänzen, ist dir Florenz verloren." Es war indes Lorenzo, der durch seine Heirat mit einer Orsini aus dem ältesten italienischen Adelsgeschlecht den Medici zum Fürstenthron verhalf. Und er war es, unter dem die Renaissance auf geradezu revolutionäre Weise Licht und Erleuchtung in die Düsternis des ausgehenden Mittelalters brachte und in Florenz eine beispiellose kulturelle Blüte entfalten konnte, auch wenn die gesellschaftlichen Regeln streng und die Bräuche in den umliegenden ländlichen Gemeinschaften auf lange Zeit archaisch blieben.

Unter Florenz wuchs die Toskana schließlich mit allem was zu ihr gehörte an moralischen Werten, intellektueller Kraft und Überlebenswillen, zu einem Bollwerk des Geistes gegen die Faschisten heran. So verwundert es nicht, dass die braunen Barbaren des 20. Jahrhunderts,

businessman and friend of the fine arts. Beloved by the people as the leader of the opposition against the oligarchy, he laid the foundation for the might and wealth of his descendants. "We are not kings, nor princes in Florence. No parchment certifies a right to our greatness. We rule without a crown, by nature, by ourselves". Thomas Mann, in his only play 'Fiorenza', has Cosimo's grandson, the great Lorenzo de' Medici (1449–1492), known as 'Il Magnifico' (The Magnificent), say this on his deathbed to his son Piero. He then also warns him: "We became great by ourselves through diligence, through combat, through breeding: the languid throng marvelled in wonder and fell into our lap. However, such domination, my son, needs to be won each day anew. … If you think to rest, and to idly shine forth, Florence will be lost to you." It was however Lorenzo, through his marriage to an Orsini, the oldest Italian noble family, who helped the Medici family to be crowned as princes. Furthermore it was he, during the Renaissance, who brought light and enlightenment in a really revolutionary way into the darkness of the fading medieval era and an unparalleled cultural blossoming was able to unfold in Florence, even though societal customs remained strict, and rites and rituals in the surrounding countryside communities remained archaic for a long time to come.

Under the leadership of Florence, Tuscany finally matured in moral values, intellectual power and the will to survive, all that which constituted its whole, into a bulwark of the spirit against the Fascists, with their spirit of barbarism.

parchemin ne nous garantit notre grandeur. Nous régnons sans couronne, par nature ». C'est-ce que fait dire Thomas Mann, dans la seule pièce qu'il a écrite, « Fiorenza », au petit-fils de Cosme, le grand Laurent de Médicis (1449–1492) dit le Magnifique, sur son lit de mort à son fils Pierre avant de l'avertir : « Nous sommes devenus grands, par le zèle, par la lutte, par l'éducation : la foule indolente s'en étonna et fut à nous. Mais un tel pouvoir, mon fils, doit être conquis tous les jours à nouveau… Si tu songes à te reposer et briller sans rien faire, Florence est perdue pour toi. » En attendant ce fut Laurent qui fit des Médicis des souverains, en épousant une Orsini, issue de la plus ancienne famille aristocratique italienne. Et ce fut sous son gouvernement que la Renaissance apporta de manière quasi révolutionnaire la lumière dans les ténèbres du Moyen Age finissant, et put générer un épanouissement culturel sans pareil à Florence, même si les conventions sociales étaient sévères et si les coutumes restèrent longtemps archaïques dans les communes paysannes des alentours.

Sous Florence finalement, la Toscane, forte de toutes ses valeurs morales, de sa puissance intellectuelle et de sa volonté de survivre, se transforma en un bastion de l'esprit contre le fascisme et la barbarie. Rien d'étonnant donc si les barbares du 20e siècle, les nazis, ne surent que faire de la ville sinon la brutaliser sans rime ni raison – et sans grandes conséquences, heureusement. En 1944 alors que les troupes américaines se rapprochaient, les occupants allemands décidèrent d'emporter une partie des trésors

que se alternaron tanto buenas como malas épocas, habría de ser gobernada por una gran familia: los Médicis. Éstos no se andaban con remilgos cuando se trataba de hacer prevalecer sus intereses y no tenían reparo alguno en valerse de manipulaciones o aun cosas peores si ello les era útil o veían amenazado su poder. El primer Médici fue Cósimo el Viejo (1389–1464), un comerciante genial y amigo de las bellas artes. Era muy apreciado por el pueblo como jefe de la oposición contra la oligarquía, y fue él quien sentó las bases del poder y la fortuna de sus descendientes. En "Fiorenza", la única obra dramática que nos legara Thomas Mann, el nieto de Cósimo, el gran Lorenzo de Médici (1449–1492), llamado "el Magnífico", en su lecho de muerte le dice a su hijo Piero: "No somos reyes, no somos príncipes en Florencia. Ningún pergamino nos documenta nuestra grandeza. Gobernamos sin corona, porque es nuestra naturaleza, porque somos así". Luego, más adelante, le advierte: "Nos hicimos grandes gracias al trabajo, a la lucha y a la disciplina. Ante ello, la masa indolente se quedó pasmada, y nos tocó guiarla. Pero esta autoridad, hijo mío, hay que ganársela de nuevo día tras día. ... Si piensas que puedes dormirte sobre tus laureles y brillar cruzándote de brazos, perderás Florencia". No obstante, fue Lorenzo quien les proporcionó a los Médicis el trono principesco en virtud de su matrimonio con una Orsini, miembro del más antiguo linaje noble de Italia. Y fue bajo su gobierno que el renacimiento, de una manera francamente revolucionaria, llevó luz y esclarecimiento a la oscuridad que existía en las postrimerías del medioevo, y contribuyó así a que en Florencia se produjera un

ricchezza dei suoi discendenti. "Non siamo re né principi di Firenze. La nostra grandezza non è sancita da nessuna pergamena. Siamo dominatori per nascita, per natura", fa dire Thomas Mann al nipote di Cosimo, il grande Lorenzo de' Medici (1449–1492) detto "il Magnifico", nella sua unica opera teatrale "Fiorenza", parlando al figlio Piero dal suo letto di morte. Lorenzo poi ammonisce: "Abbiamo conquistato la grandezza con il lavoro, la lotta, la disciplina: la massa indolente stupì e venne a noi. Ma questa forza di dominio, figlio mio, dev'essere conquistata giorno per giorno. ... Se pensi di fermarti e di brillare nell'ozio Firenze per te sarà perduta." Ma fu proprio Lorenzo che, grazie alle sue nozze con una Orsini proveniente dalla più antica dinastia della nobiltà italiana, conquistò ai Medici il trono principesco. E fu con lui che il Rinascimento, in modo addirittura rivoluzionario, gettò luce e splendore nelle tenebre del Medioevo ormai alla fine dando vita a Firenze a una fioritura culturale senza precedenti, sebbene le regole della società e le usanze delle comunità delle campagne limitrofe siano rimaste a lungo arcaiche.

Sotto la guida di Firenze la Toscana, con tutti i suoi valori morali, la sua forza intellettuale e il suo istinto di sopravvivenza, divenne infine un bastione dello spirito antifascista opponendosi alla barbarie. Non sorprende dunque che la brutalità nazista non fu in grado di opporre nulla a questa città se non una violenza insensata che fortunatamente rimase in gran parte senza effetto. Mentre nel 1944, le forze armate statunitensi si avvicinavano, gli occupanti tedeschi vollero portar via una parte dei tesori

die Nationalsozialisten, nichts weiter mit der Stadt anzufangen wussten, außer ihr sinnlos Gewalt anzutun. Zum Glück weitgehend vergeblich. Als 1944 die US-Streitkräfte näher rückten, wollten die deutschen Besatzer einen Teil der Kunstschätze fortschaffen, welche Anna Maria Ludovika, die letzte Nachfahrin von Cosimo dem Älteren, 1743 dem Staat unter der Bedingung vermacht hatte, dass kein Stück jemals Florenz verlassen dürfe und alles stets der Öffentlichkeit zugänglich sein müsse. Zum Glück hatten die Deutschen keine Transportmittel mehr zur Verfügung. Und so blieb alles dort, wo es hingehörte. Dennoch konnten die verbrecherischen Befehlshaber der „Wehrmacht“ ihren niederen Instinkten nicht widerstehen, als sie bei ihrem Rückzug meinten, wenigstens alle Brücken über den Arno sprengen zu müssen. Immerhin, die ebenfalls verminte Ponte Vecchio blieb auf Befehl des Generalfeldmarschalls Kesselring, eines Einäugigen unter Blinden, verschont.

Nach dem Krieg erblühte Florenz allmählich wieder in alter Pracht und Würde und in architektonischer Strenge. Und mit der Stadt erblühte auch die Toskana von neuem, feierte Wiederauferstehung von der Geschichte mit ihren Geschichten und großen Namen. Bald setzte allerdings auch etwas ein, was es vorher nicht gab: ein nicht mehr abebbender Strom des gehobenen Massentourismus. Wobei die Kombination der kulinarischen Überraschungen mit den Kunst-Genüssen der Landschaft, diese absolute Harmonie von leiblicher und geistiger Kost ein verführerisches Lockmittel war – und ist. So wandelte sich die Toskana

So it is of no surprise that the black-shirt Barbarians of the 20th century, the National Socialists, were incapable of achieving anything within the city except to exert their senseless violence. Fortunately they were for the most part unsuccessful. In 1944, as US forces drew nearer, the German occupying forces intended to take away some of the art treasures that Anna Maria Ludovica, the last descendent of Cosimo de' Medici, bequeathed to the state in 1743 on condition that not one piece should ever be allowed to leave Florence and all art objects should always be accessible to the public. Fortunately, the Germans did not have sufficient transport available, and thus all the treasures remained there where they belong. Nevertheless, the criminal commanders of the 'wehrmacht' could not resist their lowest instincts, and at the moment of their retreat they determined that they must at least blow up all the bridges across the Arno. Ultimately, the Ponte Vecchio, which had also been set with explosives, remained intact on the order of Field Marshal Kesselring, the only one-eyed man among the blind.

After the war, Florence finally blossomed once again in its old splendour and majesty and under a policy of architectural austerity. Furthermore, along with the city, Tuscany also blossomed once again in a new, festive resurgence from history with its stories and great names. However, there soon occurred something which had not existed before: An unabating current of 'superior' mass tourism. Although, the combination of culinary surprises with the art pleasures of the landscape, this absolute harmony of

artistiques qu'Anna Maria Ludovica, la dernière descendante de Cosme l'Ancien avait légués à l'Etat à la condition qu'aucune pièce ne quitterait jamais Florence et que tout resterait constamment accessible au public. Par bonheur, les Allemands ne disposaient plus de moyens de transport – et tout resta à sa place. Il n'empêche qu'en se repliant les commandants criminels de la Wehrmacht ne purent surmonter leurs bas instincts et voulurent faire au moins sauter tous les ponts de l'Arno. Le Ponte Vecchio, lui aussi miné, ne fut épargné que sur l'ordre du Maréchal Kesselring, un borgne au pays des aveugles.

La guerre terminée, Florence a retrouvé progressivement son ancienne splendeur, sa dignité et sa rigueur architecturale. Et la Toscane de s'épanouir à nouveau à l'instar de sa capitale, fêtant sa résurrection historique avec des histoires et de grands noms. Toutefois on assiste bientôt à l'émergence d'un phénomène inédit, l'apparition d'un flot continu de touristes haut-de-gamme. Il faut dire que le mariage de surprises gastronomiques et de jouissances artistiques et paysagères, cette harmonie absolue de nourritures terrestres et spirituelles est un appât irrésistible. Ainsi, de Florence à Pienza en passant par Sienne, de San Gimignano à Arezzo, de Pise à Lucques et Carrare au nord et à l'île d'Elbe au sud, la Toscane est devenue un paysage culturel européen unique en son genre, peut-être le plus grand musée de plein air de l'histoire de l'art. Chacun de ses pas entraîne l'habitant ou le voyageur au moyen âge, à l'époque romane et gothique, le fait passer de la Renaissance à la période romantique, du baroque au

florecimiento cultural sin precedentes a pesar de que las normas sociales continuaron siendo severas y las costumbres en las comunidades rurales vecinas mantuvieron su carácter arcaico durante mucho tiempo.

Bajo el dominio de Florencia, la Toscana creció –con todo lo que formaba parte de ella: los valores morales, la fuerza intelectual y la voluntad de sobrevivir– hasta convertirse en un baluarte del espíritu contra la barbarie de los fascistas. Por ello no sorprende que a los bárbaros "camisas marrones" del siglo XX, es decir, a los nacionalsocialistas, no se les ocurriera qué hacer con la ciudad aparte de infligirle violencia sin sentido. Felizmente sus acciones no ocasionaron daños dignos de mención. Cuando en 1944 las fuerzas armadas estadounidenses se estaban acercando, los invasores alemanes quisieron llevarse una parte de los tesoros artísticos que Ana María Ludovica, la última descendiente de Cósimo el Viejo, había legado a la ciudad, en 1743, bajo la condición de que ninguna pieza abandonara jamás Florencia y de que el público siempre tuviera acceso a ellas. Por fortuna los alemanes ya no disponían de medios de transporte. Y así todo permaneció donde debía quedarse. A pesar de ello, en el momento cuando abandonaban la ciudad, los criminales comandantes de la Wehrmacht no pudieron resistir sus bajos instintos y no se les ocurrió mejor idea que la de hacer volar, por lo menos, todos los puentes sobre el río Arno. No obstante, el Ponte Vecchio, al que también habían minado, se salvó por orden del mariscal de campo Kesselring, un tuerto entre los ciegos.

artistici che erano stati donati alla città da Anna Maria Ludovica, l'ultima discendente di Cosimo il Vecchio, a condizione che nessuna opera lasciasse mai Firenze e che tutte fossero sempre accessibili al pubblico. Per fortuna i tedeschi non avevano più mezzi di trasporto a loro disposizione. Così tutto rimase al suo posto. Tuttavia i criminali che comandavano la "Wehrmacht" non seppero resistere ai propri istinti più bassi e, nel ritirarsi, decisero di far saltare tutti i ponti sull'Arno. Almeno il Ponte Vecchio, che pure era stato minato, rimase intatto per ordine del Feldmaresciallo Kesselring, che manifestò un pizzico di umanità in più rispetto agli altri gerarchi.

Dopo la guerra Firenze rifiorì gradualmente nel rigore architettonico fino allo splendore e alla dignità di una volta. Insieme alla città rifiorì anche la Toscana che celebrò la rinascita della sua storia, delle sue storie, dei suoi grandi nomi. Presto tuttavia ebbe inizio un fenomeno mai visto prima: un flusso inarrestabile di turisti di massa di buon livello. Polo di attrazione e seduzione era ed è ancora quella combinazione di sorprese gastronomiche e di godimento artistico e paesaggistico, quell'assoluta armonia tra piaceri del corpo e dello spirito. La Toscana, da Firenze a Pienza passando per Siena, da San Gimignano ad Arezzo, da Pisa a Lucca e a Carrara nel nord e all'isola d'Elba ad ovest, si trasformò così in una sorta di straordinario parco culturale europeo e forse nel più grande museo all'aria aperta nella storia dell'arte: a ogni pie' sospinto chiunque, residente o viaggiatore, si trova qui in un continuo viaggio nel tempo attraverso il Medioevo romanico e gotico, per

von Florenz über Siena bis Pienza, von San Gimignano bis Arrezo, von Pisa über Lucca, hinauf nach Carrara und nach Süden, bis hinüber nach Elba, zu einer einzigartigen europäischen Kultur-Parklandschaft, ja vielleicht zum größten Freilichtmuseum der Kunstgeschichte: Auf Schritt und Tritt befindet sich jeder, ob Einwohner oder Reisender, auf einer Zeitreise durch das Mittelalter, die Romanik und die Gotik, wechselt er von der Renaissance in die Romantik, vom Barock hinein in den Manierismus, verweilt in der Strenge des Klassizismus oder im modernistisch verspielten Jugendstil.

Selten hat sich über Jahrhunderte in einer Region soviel Prominenz aus der Welt der Architektur, der Malerei, der Literatur und Dichtung, der Politik und Wirtschaft in Stein, auf Leinwand und Papier versammelt und verewigt wie hier. Dazu passt es, dass ausgerechnet in dem Dörfchen Vinci bei Florenz im Jahre 1452, dem Todesjahr von Lorenzo dem Prächtigen, ein gewisser Leonardo als unehelicher Sohn einer Bäuerin und eines Florentiner Notars zur Welt kam. Er sollte als Kuriosität und Genie gleichermaßen verblüffen: Leonardo da Vinci, der Maler der „Mona Lisa" und des „Abendmahls", ein Bildhauer, Musiker und Poet, Philosoph und Astronom, Optiker, Mathematiker, Physiker und Meteorologe, Biologe und Anatom, ein Ingenieur und Architekt, Festungsbaumeister und Kriegswaffenkonstrukteur. Er war seiner Zeit weit voraus und schlug mit seinen genialen Ideen, Erfindungen und Träumen weitsichtig eine Brücke in unsere Gegenwart.

corporeal and spiritual fare, was a seductive lure – and still is. Thus Tuscany, from Florence via Siena to Pienza, from San Gimignano to Arezzo, from Pisa via Lucca, up to Carrara and to the south, and across to Elba, transformed into a unique European culture-park landscape, even perhaps into the greatest open-air museum in the history of art: Whether resident or traveller, at every turn each and everyone will find themselves on a journey through time, through the Middle Ages, the Romanesque and the Gothic, changing from the Renaissance into Romanticism, from Baroque and into Mannerism, pausing in the austerity of Classicism or in playfully modernist Art Nouveau.

Other than here in Tuscany, only seldom have so many prominent individuals from the world of architecture, painting, literature and poetry, of politics and economy, converged upon a region over centuries and immortalised themselves in stone, on canvas and on paper. It is fitting then, that of all places, in the little village of Vinci near Florence in 1452 a certain Leonardo was born as an illegitimate son of a farm girl and a Florentine notary. He was to amaze everyone as a curiosity and equally as a genius: Leonardo da Vinci, the painter of the 'Mona Lisa' and of the 'Last Supper', a sculptor, musician and poet, philosopher and astronomer, optician, mathematician, physicist and meteorologist, biologist and anatomist, engineer and architect, master builder of fortresses and creator of weapons of war. He was far ahead of his time and he sagaciously built a bridge to our modern times with his ingenious ideas, inventions and dreams.

maniérisme, le fait suspendre sa marche pour contempler la sévérité néoclassique ou le ludisme de l'Art nouveau.

Il est rare qu'une région ait réuni au cours des siècles autant de personnalités du monde de l'architecture, de la peinture, de la littérature et de la poésie, de la politique et de l'économie, qui se sont immortalisées dans la pierre, sur la toile et le papier. Ainsi c'est justement dans le petit village de Vinci près de Florence qu'est né en 1452 un certain Léonard, fils illégitime d'une paysanne et d'un notaire florentin. Il stupéfiera le monde, autant par son génie que son originalité prodigieuse : Léonard de Vinci, le peintre de « La Joconde » et de « La Cène », sculpteur, musicien et poète, philosophe et astronome, opticien, mathématicien, physicien et météorologue, biologiste et anatomiste, ingénieur et architecte, bâtisseur de forteresses et constructeur d'armes de guerre. Très en avance sur son temps, ce visionnaire a jeté un pont vers notre époque avec ses idées extraordinaires, ses inventions et ses rêves.

Piero della Francesca (1414–1492), maître du début de la Renaissance, et qui vécut à peu près à la même époque que Léonard de Vinci, est lui aussi un enfant de la Toscane. Un demi-millénaire plus tard, ses fresques influenceront des peintres du 20e siècle comme Max Beckmann et Pablo Picasso. Dante Alighieri (1265–1321), Francesco Petrarca dit Pétrarque (1304–1374) et son élève Giovanni Boccaccio dit Boccace (1313–1375) font également partie de ces esprits hors du commun. L'œuvre de ces poètes maudits, persécutés et admirés embrasse la période qui

Después de la guerra, Florencia poco a poco empezó a florecer nuevamente con su antiguo esplendor, dignidad y severidad arquitectónica. Y junto con la ciudad, también empezó a florecer nuevamente la Toscana, la cual celebró su resurrección en la Historia con sus historias y sus grandes nombres. Sin embargo, muy pronto también comenzó a manifestarse un fenómeno que antes no había existido, a saber, la llegada de un raudal incontenible de turismo de masas ilustrado cada vez más abundante. Aunque, a decir verdad, la combinación de las sorpresas culinarias con los goces artísticos del paisaje, esta armonía absoluta de alimento espiritual y físico, siempre fue –y será– un seductor medio de atracción. Desde Florencia, pasando por Siena, hasta Pienza, desde San Gimignano hasta Arezzo, desde Pisa, pasando por Lucca, yendo al norte hasta Carrara y hacia el sur hasta llegar a la isla de Elba, la Toscana se transformó en un gran parque cultural europeo sin par, quizás, incluso, en el más grande museo al aire libre de historia del arte: a cada paso se encuentra uno, sea habitante del lugar o viajero, en un viaje a través del tiempo por la Edad Media, el románico y el gótico; puede cambiar del renacimiento al romanticismo o ir del barroco directamente al manierismo; o tal vez quiera detenerse frente a la severidad del clasicismo o frente al modernismo juguetón del Art Nouveau.

Pocas veces ha ocurrido que en una sola región se hayan congregado y perennizado en la piedra, el lienzo o el papel tantas celebridades del mundo de la arquitectura, de la pintura, de la prosa y la poesía, de la política y la economía

passare poi dal Rinascimento al Romanticismo, dal Barocco fino al Manierismo e infine sostare nella sobrietà del Neoclassicismo o nella giocosa modernità del Liberty.

In pochi luoghi si è verificato nei secoli l'accumulo di grandi opere architettoniche, pittoriche, letterarie, poetiche, politiche ed economiche, immortalato nella pietra, su tela o carta, come è accaduto in Toscana. Non è forse un caso che proprio nel villaggio di Vinci, presso Firenze, nel 1452 sia nato un certo Leonardo, figlio illegittimo di una contadina e di un notaio fiorentino. Un personaggio sorprendente, a metà tra genio e fenomeno da baraccone: Leonardo da Vinci, autore della "Gioconda" e dell'"Ultima cena", scultore, musicista e poeta, filosofo ed astronomo, ottico, matematico, fisico e meteorologo, biologo e anatomista, ingegnere ed architetto, costruttore di fortificazioni e armi da guerra. Fu in largo anticipo sui suoi tempi e con le sue idee, le sue invenzioni, le sue visioni geniali costruì un ponte di lungimiranza tra la sua epoca e i nostri giorni.

Un "figlio" della Toscana di genere diverso fu il maestro del primo Rinascimento Piero della Francesca, vissuto all'incirca nella stessa epoca di Leonardo (1414–1492) e i cui affreschi, mezzo millennio dopo, influenzarono pittori del XX secolo come Max Beckmann e Pablo Picasso. Anche la triade poetica formata da Dante Alighieri (1265–1321), Francesco Petrarca (1304–1374) e dal suo allievo Giovanni Boccaccio (1313–1375) conferma la grandezza dello spirito toscano. Essa fu maledetta, perseguitata ma

Ein „Kind“ der Toskana anderer Art war der Meister der Frührenaissance Piero della Francesca, der etwa zur selben Zeit wie Leonardo lebte (1414–1492) und dessen Fresken ein halbes Jahrtausend später Maler des 20. Jahrhunderts wie Max Beckmann und Pablo Picasso beeinflussten. Auch das Dichter-Triumvirat Dante Alighieri (1265–1321), Francesco Petrarca (1304–1374) und dessen Schüler Giovanni Boccaccio (1313–1375) gehört zu diesen genialen Geistesgrößen. Verdammt, verfolgt und bewundert schlug es den dichterischen Spannungsbogen vom ausgehenden 13. Jahrhundert zum Ende des 14. Jahrhunderts und wird auch im 20. Jahrhundert noch verehrt.

Zwar hat die Medaille auch ihre Kehrseite, wenn nämlich die auf die Medici gefolgten Fremdenverkehrsmanager heute jedem Quadratmeter Boden, jedem Meter Weg, zahllosem Gemäuer, manchmal selbst solchem von profaner Wertlosigkeit, aus vordergründigem pekuniärem Interesse eine historische Bedeutung beimessen. Doch wer bei der Wanderung durch die Uffizien, die Gassen von San Gimignano oder Siena im Touristengewühl gar das Privileg hat, dort – rund um den Campo, den traditionellen Palio – den mittelalterlichen Reiterwettstreit der 17 Stadtviertel, der Contrade, zu erleben, für den verflüchtigt sich der merkantile Beigeschmack. Und da die Regierung immerhin mit strengen Gesetzen darüber wacht, dass die Landschaft nicht mit ambitionierten Großprojekten zu Tode zersiedelt wird, konnte die physiognomische Ursprünglichkeit und Wiedererkennbarkeit dieser Kulturlandschaft bewahrt werden. So ist es auch heute möglich,

A ‘child’ of Tuscany of another sort was the master of the early renaissance Piero della Francesca who lived at about the same time as Leonardo (1414–1492) and whose frescos influenced 20th century painters – such as Max Beckmann and Pablo Picasso – half a millennium later. The poet-triumvirate of Dante Alighieri (1265–1321), Francesco Petrarch (1304–1374) and his pupil Giovanni Boccaccio (1313–1375) also belonged to these ingenious and great spirits. Damned, persecuted and venerated, this poetical arc of tension spanned from the outgoing 13th century to the end of the 14th century and is still revered today.

Indeed, the coin has its reverse side, when namely tourist managers of today, as the successors to the Medici spirit, attach historic importance to each square foot of floor, each yard of pathway, countless old piles of masonry, sometimes even of such profane trashiness, out of obvious pecuniary interest. Although, whoever experiences a stroll through the halls of the Uffizi, or the alleyways of San Gimignano, or has the privilege of Siena’s tourist-bustle all around the Campo during the traditional Palio – the medieval horse race between the 17 city contrade (districts) – then the smell of mercantilism will somewhat evaporate. Furthermore, since the government ensures with strict laws that the landscape does not become hideously redeveloped with ambitious large-scale building projects anyway, the physiognomic originality and recognisable identity of this cultural landscape has been successfully retained. It is thus also possible today, to experience Tuscany as in a daydream, to explore it on foot,

va de la fin du 13e siècle à la fin du 14e siècle et est encore vénérée aujourd'hui.

Toute médaille a son revers et il est vrai que les managers du tourisme qui ont suivi les Médicis accordent aujourd'hui à chaque mètre carré du sol, à chaque mètre de chemin, à d'innombrables murs, quelquefois même à ceux qui n'ont aucune valeur profane, une signification historique, et ce surtout par intérêt financier. Mais pour celui qui a le privilège, au milieu de la foule des touristes, de traverser les Offices, de parcourir les ruelles de San Gimignano ou d'assister au Palio – une course de chevaux datant du moyen âge, que se disputent les dix-sept quartiers de la ville, les contrade –, qui se déroule à Sienne autour de la place du Campo, pour celui-là dont, l'arrière-goût de mercantilisme se dissipe. Le gouvernement veillant à l'aide de lois sévères à ce que le paysage ne soit pas urbanisé à mort par d'ambitieux projets de développement, ce paysage culturel a pu conserver son originalité d'aspect et est resté reconnaissable entre tous. Ainsi il est aujourd'hui encore possible de vivre la Toscane comme un rêve éveillé, de l'explorer à pied, en bicyclette ou en voiture. Assis sur une colline dans un hôtel près de Sienne, dans une trattoria à Greve ou se reposant dans un café sur les remparts après une promenade à travers Pienza, cette petite ville modèle de la Renaissance commandée par le pape Pie II au 15e siècle et édifiée à la place de son village natal Corsignano, le voyageur contemple le paysage qui s'offre à lui. Il a sous les yeux des images semblables à celles qu' Axel M. Mosler a photographiées pour le présent ouvrage.

a lo largo de los siglos como aquí. En este sentido viene muy a propósito que precisamente en el pueblecito de Vinci, cerca de Florencia, un tal Leonardo, hijo ilegítimo de una campesina y de un notario florentino, viera la luz del día en 1452. Éste habría de causar estupefacción no sólo por su singularidad, sino también por su genialidad: Leonardo da Vinci, el pintor de la "Mona Lisa" y de "La última cena", escultor, músico y poeta, filósofo y astrónomo, óptico, matemático, físico y meteorólogo, biólogo y anatomista, ingeniero y arquitecto, maestro de obras de fortalezas y constructor de armas bélicas. Era un adelantado de su tiempo, y con sus geniales ideas, inventos y sueños, tendió previsoramente un puente hasta nuestros días.

Un "hijo" de la Toscana, de otro tipo, fue Piero della Francesca (1414–1492), maestro del renacimiento temprano, quien vivió más o menos en la misma época que Leonardo y cuyos frescos influyeron, medio milenio más tarde, en la obra de algunos pintores del siglo XX como, por ejemplo, Max Beckmann y Pablo Picasso. También el triunvirato de poetas constituido por Dante Alighieri (1265–1321), Francesco Petrarca (1304–1374) y su discípulo Giovanni Boccaccio (1313–1375) forman parte de estos preclaros espíritus geniales. Maldecidos, perseguidos y admirados, esta tríada tiende el arco de tensión poético desde las postrimerías del siglo XIII hasta finales del XIV, y se los venera también hoy.

Bien es verdad que la moneda tiene otra cara, la misma que sale a relucir cuando los empresarios del turismo, que

anche ammirata. Formò un arco poetico tra la fine del XIII e la fine del XIV secolo ed è ancora oggi oggetto di venerazione.

Certo, la medaglia ha anche il suo rovescio, ad esempio quegli operatori turistici succeduti ai Medici che oggi, per interessi soprattutto pecuniari, attribuiscono importanza storica a ogni metro quadrato di terreno, a ogni metro di strada e ad ogni costruzione, anche quando sia completamente priva di valore. Eppure chi abbia il privilegio, attraversando le sale degli Uffizi, passeggiando per i vicoli di San Gimignano oppure, nella massa di turisti intorno al Campo, di assistere al tradizionale Palio medievale delle diciassette Contrade di Siena, non sentirà più quel retrogusto mercantile. E grazie all'opera di un governo che veglia con leggi severissime affinché il paesaggio toscano non venga rovinato da grandi e ambiziosi progetti edilizi, è stato possibile mantenere la fisionomia originale e riconoscibile di questa terra di cultura. Ancora oggi è possibile vivere la Toscana come un sogno ad occhi aperti ed esplorarla a piedi, in bicicletta o in auto. Sia che il viaggiatore si trovi in un hotel di campagna situato in cima a una colle senese, in una trattoria di Greve oppure, dopo una passeggiata verso Pienza, la piccola città ideale commissionata da Papa Pio II nel XV secolo sul luogo in cui sorgeva il villaggio natale di Corsignano, in un caffè sulle mura di cinta osservando la campagna dei dintorni, davanti ai suoi occhi ci saranno le stesse immagini che Axel M. Mosler ha catturato nelle fotografie contenute in questo libro.

die Toskana wie in einem Tagtraum zu erleben, sie zu Fuß, per Fahrrad oder Auto zu erkunden. Sitzt der Reisende dann auf einem Hügel in einem Landhotel bei Siena, in einer Trattoria in Greve oder nach dem Spaziergang durch Pienza, die kleine, von Papst Pius II. im 15. Jahrhundert in Auftrag gegebene und an der Stelle seines Heimatdorfes Corsignano errichtete Idealstadt der Renaissance, in einem Café auf der Stadtmauer und lässt den Blick weit ins Land schweifen, so stehen ihm Bilder vor Augen, wie sie Axel M. Mosler in seinen Photographien für diesen Band eingefangen hat.

by bike or by car. If the traveller then sits down in a country hotel on a hilltop near Siena, or in a trattoria in Greve, or after wandering through Pienza – the little town constructed by order of Pope Pius II in the 15th century on the site of his hometown Corsignano, as the ideal Renaissance town – sits down in a cafe on the city walls and lets his or her gaze wander far across the landscape, then images will appear just like those by Axel M. Mosler, captured in his photographs for this volume.

sucedieron a los Médicis, motivados sólo por el evidente interés pecuniario, le atribuyen un significado histórico a cada metro cuadrado de suelo, a cada centímetro del camino, a innumerables murallas, a veces incluso a aquellas cargadas de profana futilidad. Sin embargo, quien durante su recorrido por la Galería de los Oficios, por las estrechas callecitas de San Gimignano o de Siena, en medio del hervidero de turistas, incluso tenga el privilegio de ser testigo en esta última del certamen ecuestre medieval –el tradicional Palio– que se realiza alrededor de la Piazza del Campo y en el que participan los 17 distritos de la ciudad, los Contrade, dejará de percibir ese resabio mercantil. Y como, además, el Gobierno vela con leyes estrictas para evitar que grandes y ambiciosos proyectos destruyan el paisaje hasta darle muerte urbanizándolo, se ha podido mantener la fisonomía original y reconocible de este paisaje cultural. Por ello es que hoy también es posible ver y percibir la Toscana como en un sueño diurno, y de viajar por ella, explorándola y descubriéndola, a pie, en bicicleta o en coche. Si el viajero está sentado en un hotel campestre que se levanta sobre una colina cerca de Siena o en una trattoria en Greve o si, después de dar un paseo por Pienza, la pequeña "ciudad ideal del Renacimiento" construida por encargo del Papa Pío II en el siglo XV en el lugar que había ocupado Corsignano, su pueblo natal, toma asiento en un café en lo alto de las murallas de la ciudad y pasea la mirada escrutando esta región hasta el horizonte, tendrá imágenes ante sus ojos como las que ha captado Axel M. Mosler en las fotografías que aparecen en este volumen.

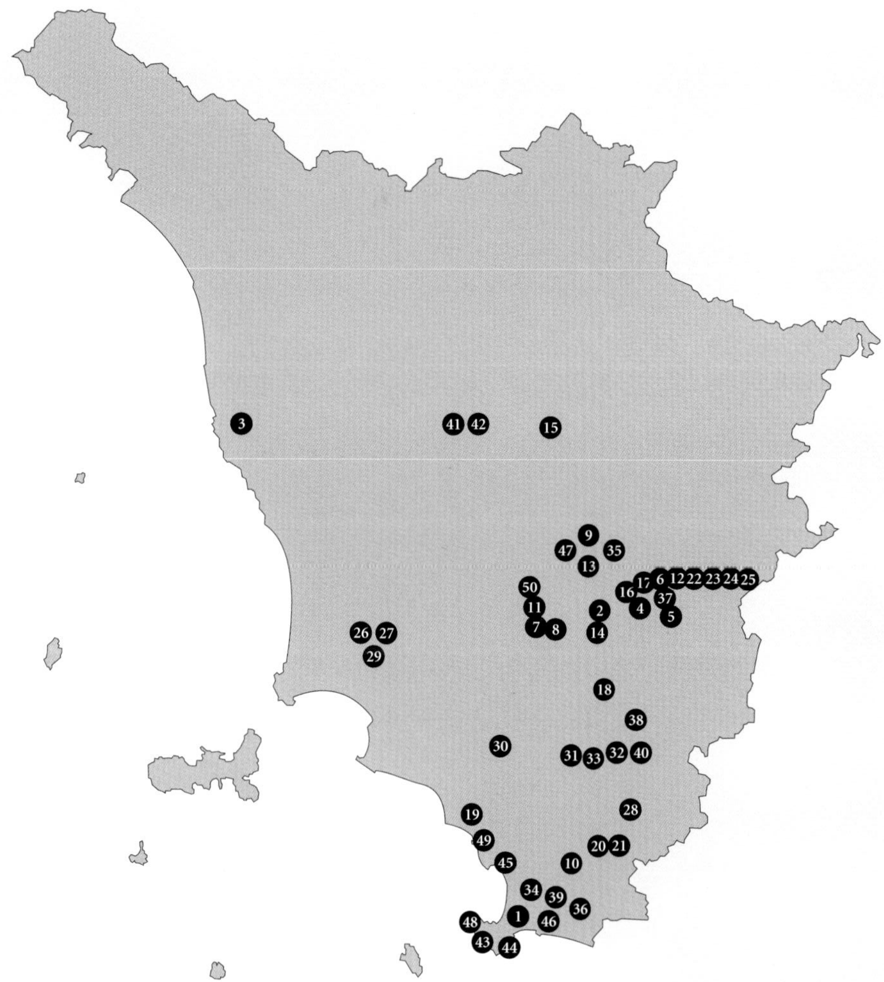
1
2
3
4
5
6
7
8
9
10
11
12
13
14
15
16
17
18
19
20
21
22
23
24
25
26
27
28
29
30
31
32
33
34
35
36
37
38
39
40
41
42
43
44
45
46
47
48
49
50

1 Orbetello presso Monte Argentario

2 Presso San Quirico d’Orcia

▶ 3 Pisa

4 Presso Pienza

► 5 Presso Monticchiello

6 San Biagio presso Montepulciano

7 Montalcino

8 Castello di Montalcino

► 9 Asciano, Crete

10 Presso Manciano

11 Montalcino

ZENITH
SALVIONI Audio Video
FARMACIA

12 Torre Tarugi presso La Foce

13 Monte Oliveto Maggiore

14 Bagno Vignoni

▸ 15 Presso Radda, Chianti

16 Pienza

17 Pienza

18 Presso Monte Amiata

▸ **19** Maremma

21 Pitigliano

23 Montepulciano

▸ 25 Montepulciano

26 Plaza, Siena

▸ 27 Siena

28 Sorano

29 Ponte d'Arbia

30 Presso Grosseto

31 Presso Radicofani

▸ 32 Presso Radicofani

33 Castello Radicofani

34 Viale Maremma

35 Presso Monte Oliveto Maggiore

▸ 36 Farnese

37 Monticchiello

VIA
DI
MEZZO
ALTROIERI

38 Presso Monte Amiata

39 Maremma

▸ 41 Firenze

42 Ponte Vecchio, Firenze

▸ 43 Monte Argentario

44 Porto Ercole, Monte Argentario

45 Maremma

46 Maremma

47 Crete

▸ **48** Porto Santo Stefano

49 Maremma

▸ **50** Presso Montalcino

AXEL M. MOSLER wurde 1953 in Dortmund geboren, wo er auch sein Fachhochschulstudium der Photographie absolvierte. Seit 1977 ist er als freier Photo-Designer und Landschaftsphotograph tätig. Panoramaphotographie ist fester Bestandteil seiner photographischen Arbeit, die nicht nur in zahlreichen Bildbänden renommierter Verlage vorliegt, sondern auch auf vielen Ausstellungen im In- und Ausland gezeigt wird. Ausgedehnte Photoreisen haben ihn unter anderem nach Schottland, Norwegen, Kanada, Griechenland und in die Toskana geführt.

VOLKER SKIERKA wurde 1952 in Rheinfelden/Baden geboren. Nach seiner journalistischen Ausbildung war er zunächst für die Nachrichtenagentur Reuters tätig, danach bis 1992 für die „Süddeutsche Zeitung“, zuletzt als Lateinamerikakorrespondent. Bis 1997 war er Chefredakteur des Kultur- und Reisemagazins „Merian“ und arbeitet seitdem als freier Publizist für Buchverlage, Zeitungen, Zeitschriften und Fernsehproduktionen. Volker Skierka hat zahlreiche Auszeichnungen für seine Arbeit erhalten, darunter den Egon-Erwin-Kisch-Preis im Jahre 1981. Seine Biographie über Fidel Castro gilt als Standardwerk. Volker Skierka lebt und arbeitet in Hamburg.

AXEL M. MOSLER was born in 1953 in Dortmund, where he also graduated from his photographic studies at the technical high school. Since 1977 he has been active as a freelance photo-designer and landscape photographer. Panorama photography is a permanent feature of his photographic work which is not only available in many illustrated volumes from renowned publishers, but is also presented at many exhibitions at home and abroad. Extensive photographic expeditions have taken him to Scotland, Norway, Canada, Greece and Tuscany among others.

VOLKER SKIERKA was born in 1952 in Rheinfelden/Baden. After his training as a journalist, he first worked for the “Reuters” news agency and later for the “Süddeutsche Zeitung” whose correspondent for Latin America he was until 1992. Through 1997 he was editor in chief of the culture and travel magazine “Merian” and he has been working as a freelance journalist for publishing houses, newspapers, magazines, and television ever since. Volker Skierka has received numerous awards for his work, the Egon-Erwin-Kisch-Prize in 1981 amongst them. His biography about Fidel Castro is widely seen to be the work of reference on the subject. Volker Skierka lives and works in Hamburg.

AXEL M. MOSLER est né en 1953 à Dortmund, où il a fait des études supérieures de photographie. Depuis 1977 il travaille comme photo-designer indépendant et photographe paysager. Les panoramas qu'il photographie régulièrement ne sont pas seulement présentés dans les nombreux livres de photographies d'éditeurs réputés mais aussi dans de nombreuses expositions nationales et internationales. Les longs voyages entrepris dans le cadre de son travail l'ont conduit entre autres en Ecosse, en Norvège, au Canada, en Grèce et en Toscane.

VOLKER SKIERKA est né en 1952 à Rheinfelden/Baden. Après une formation de journaliste, il a tout d'abord travaillé pour l'agence de presse « Reuters » et ensuite pour le journal « Süddeutsche Zeitung » dont il a été correspondant en Amérique latine jusqu'en 1992. Jusqu'en 1997 il a été rédacteur en chef de la revue « Merian » (culture et voyages) et travaille depuis en indépendant pour de nombreux éditeurs, pour la presse écrite et pour la télévision. Volker Skierka a obtenu de nombreux prix pour son œuvre, dont le « Egon-Erwin-Kisch-Preis » en 1981. Sa bibliographie sur Fidel Castro est devenue un ouvrage de référence. Volker Skierka vit et travaille à Hambourg.

AXEL M. MOSLER nació en Dortmund en1953, donde también realizó sus estudios de fotografía en la Universidad de Ciencias Aplicadas. Desde 1977 trabaja como diseñador fotográfico libre y fotógrafo paisajístico. La fotografía panorámica es parte esencial de su trabajo. Estas imágenes no sólo pueden apreciarse en un gran número de volúmenes publicados por casas editoriales de prestigio, sino también en muchas exposiciones tanto del país como del extranjero. Largos y extensos viajes fotográficos lo han llevado, entre otros lugares, a Escocia, Noruega, Canadá, Grecia y la Toscana.

VOLKER SKIERKA nació en Rheinfelden/Baden en 1952. Después de su formación como periodista, trabajó primero para la agencia de noticias Reuter; después, hasta 1992, para el "Süddeutsche Zeitung"; su último cargo en ese diario fue el de corresponsal para América Latina. Fue jefe de redacción de la revista de cultura y viajes "Merian" hasta 1997. Desde entonces trabaja como periodista libre para casas editoriales, periódicos, revistas y producciones para la televisión. Volker Skierka ha sido merecedor de numerosos premios por sus trabajos, entre ellos el premio Egon-Erwin-Kisch, el año 1981. La biografía que escribió de Fidel Castro es considerada una obra de referencia. Volker Skierka vive y trabaja en Hamburgo.

AXEL M. MOSLER è nato nel 1953 a Dortmund, dove si è laureato in tecnica fotografica. Dal 1977 è attivo come designer fotografico e fotografo di paesaggi. La foto panoramica è parte essenziale del suo lavoro che, oltre ad essere pubblicato in numerosi libri di fotografia per rinomati editori, è stato esposto in molte mostre tenutesi in Germania e in altri paesi. I suoi articolati viaggi fotografici lo hanno condotto tra l'altro in Scozia, Norvegia, Canada, Grecia e Toscana.

VOLKER SKIERKA è nato nel 1952 a Rheinfelden/Baden. Dopo una formazione giornalistica ha lavorato dapprima per l'agenzia di stampa Reuters e poi, fino al 1992, per la "Süddeutsche Zeitung", da ultimo come corrispondente dall'America Latina. Fino al 1997 è stato caporedattore della rivista culturale e di viaggi "Merian" e da allora opera in qualità di pubblicista free lance per case editrici librarie, giornali, riviste e produzioni televisive. Volker Skierka ha ottenuto numerosi riconoscimenti per il suo lavoro, tra questi il Premio Egon Erwin Kisch nel 1981. La sua biografia di Fidel Castro è considerata un classico. Volker Skierka vive e lavora ad Amburgo.

ISBN: 978-3-89823-350-7

Concept: Bernhard Wipfler, Sebastian Wipfler, Marcus Bela Schmitt
Design: EDITION PANORAMA | Diana May & Designgruppe Fanz & Neumayer | Marcus Bela Schmitt
Editorial department: Dr. Michael Barchet, Wolfgang Roth
Translations: Global-Text Fachübersetzungen, Heidelberg | Mark Woolfe, Jocelyne Abarca, Dr. Maria Carasi, Sebastián González Mohíno
Seperations: EPS, Speyer
Printing: abcdruck GmbH, Heidelberg
Bookbinding: Josef Spinner Großbuchbinderei GmbH, Ottersweier

EDITION PANORAMA GmbH
G7, 14
D - 68159 Mannheim

www.editionpanorama.com

A production by EDITION**PANORAMA**